Sue Quinn

photographs by Victoria Wall Harris

hardie grant books

CONTENTS

INTRODUCTION

This book is designed to help you reduce or even eliminate the added sugar in your diet, which most of us need to do. Added sugars should make up no more than 10 per cent, but ideally less than 5 per cent, of the calories in the food and drink we consume each day. That means no more than 70g for men and 50g for women.

How you reduce your added sugar intake is up to you. Some people go cold turkey, while others gradually cut down, but whatever you choose to do there are a few things to bear in mind.

Regardless of the amount of added sugar you currently consume, cutting down might take time to get used to. For example, you might find that home-made ketchup doesn't have the same sweet appeal as the bought stuff, or that cakes made without refined sugar lack the flavour and texture of sugary versions. My advice is to stick with it, as your brain and taste buds will adjust in time. In fact, the longer you avoid added sugar, the less you notice it.

Many so-called sugar-free recipes are laden with honey, agave or other sweet syrups, which some people praise for being 'natural' and healthier than table sugar. The fact is, these syrups are still loaded with sugar, have little nutritional value and some contain high levels of fructose, which is believed by some experts to be especially bad for human health. That's why I have not included these ingredients in this book. Neither have I used sugar substitutes like stevia or xylitol. I believe if you are trying to cut down on added sugar, it's better to avoid artificial sweeteners, as they can fuel sugar cravings.

Instead of syrups or sugar substitutes, I've used dried and fresh fruit to sweeten. Fruit is full of fibre, so the sugars it contains are absorbed slowly and don't cause spikes in blood sugar levels. I've also used fruit juice as a sweetener in a handful of recipes. While fruit juice should be consumed in moderation as a drink, I believe it's fine to use in small amounts alongside fibre-rich ingredients in cooking.

Finally, a word of caution to readers with Type 1 or Type 2 diabetes: please seek medical advice before using the recipes in this book.

WHY SUGAR IS BAD FOR YOU

Glucose is the body's major fuel and is broken down from carbohydrates, a combination of sugar molecules, in the food we eat. When experts talk about over-consumption of sugar, they're referring to simple sugars like sucrose (also known as added sugar or table sugar) found in foods like baked goods, sweets, desserts, soft drinks, fruit juice, honey and syrups.

Added sugar has no nutritional value and is loaded with 'empty' calories. The more calories we consume, the more likely we are to be obese, and obesity is linked to heart disease, Type 2 diabetes, tooth decay and many other serious health conditions.

Some experts believe the fructose component of added sugar is especially harmful (see diagram below). Fruit and vegetables are a small source of fructose for most people and are full of fibre, which slows down digestion of the sugars they contain.

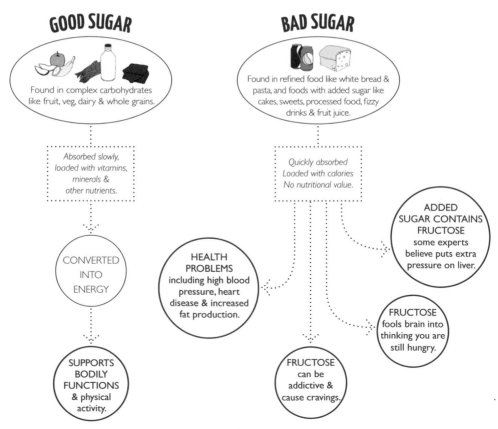

GOOD SUGAR

Found in complex carbohydrates like fruit, veg, dairy & whole grains.

Absorbed slowly, loaded with vitamins, minerals & other nutrients.

CONVERTED INTO ENERGY

SUPPORTS BODILY FUNCTIONS & physical activity.

BAD SUGAR

Found in refined food like white bread & pasta, and foods with added sugar like cakes, sweets, processed food, fizzy drinks & fruit juice.

Quickly absorbed Loaded with calories No nutritional value.

HEALTH PROBLEMS including high blood pressure, heart disease & increased fat production.

ADDED SUGAR CONTAINS FRUCTOSE some experts believe puts extra pressure on liver.

FRUCTOSE fools brain into thinking you are still hungry.

FRUCTOSE can be addictive & cause cravings.

HOW TO READ FOOD LABELS

Spotting added sugar on food labels can be difficult, but follow the tips below to avoid buying sugar-loaded products.

○ LOOK FOR sugar content under carbohydrates. It's often listed as 'carbohydrates (of which sugars)'.

○ MORE THAN 22.5g sugars per 100g is high, less than 5g of total sugars per 100g is low, and a figure in between is medium[1].

○ A LONG list of ingredients means the product is highly processed and best avoided.

FACT:

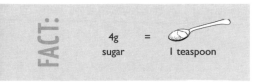

4g sugar = 1 teaspoon

○ THE FIRST 4.7g of sugar per 100ml of a dairy product is naturally occurring lactose, a good sugar – the rest is added.

○ INGREDIENTS ARE often listed in descending order by weight, so if sugar is at or near the top it's probably loaded with sugar.

○ FAMILIARISE YOURSELF with the different names for sugar on the adjacent table.

The list below contains some, but not all of the names for sugar used on food labels[2].

Agave nectar
Barbados sugar
Barley malt
Beet sugar
Blackstrap molasses
Brown sugar
Buttered syrup
Cane crystals
Caramel
Carob syrup
Confectioners' sugar
Cane juice crystals
Cane sugar
Caster sugar
Corn sweetener
Corn syrup/corn syrup solids
Crystalline fructose
Date sugar
Demerara sugar
Dextran
Dextrose
Diastatic malt
Diatase
Ethyl maltol
Evaporated cane juice
Florida crystals
Fructose
Fruit juice/fruit juice concentrates
Fruit syrup

Galactose
Glucose/glucose solids
Golden sugar
Golden syrup
Grape sugar
High-fructose corn syrup
Honey
Hydrolysed starch
Icing sugar
Invert sugar
Lactose
Maltodextrin
Maltose
Malt syrup
Maple syrup
Molasses
Muscovado sugar
Panocha
Raw sugar
Refiners' syrup
Rice syrup
Sorghum syrup
Sugar
Sucrose
Syrup
Treacle
Turbinado sugar
Yellow sugar

---

[1] NHS Choices website – How much sugar is good for me?
[2] Harvard Institute of Public Health; *Fat Chance: The bitter truth about sugar,* by Dr Robert Lustig

SMART SUGAR SWAPS

Use the table below* as a guide to replace sugar-laden products with less sugary versions. Read labels carefully, as the sugar content of a product can vary widely between brands. Also bear in mind that processed savoury food is far from sugar free. For example, 100g of barbecue crisps can contain about the same amount of added sugar as a large square of milk chocolate.

BEVERAGES (grams of sugar per 330ml serve)

	Avoid			Choose	
	fruit flavoured drink (less than 3% juice)	53g		whole milk	17g (lactose)
	mango smoothie	41g		vegetable juice	11g
	carbonated cola	36g		tomato juice	9g
	unsweetened apple juice	33g		tea, coffee, herbal tea, still & sparkling water	0g
	carbonated ginger ale	29g			

JAMS, SPREADS & CONFECTIONARY (grams of sugar per 100g)

	Avoid			Choose	
	honey	82g		mashed banana	12g
	chocolate flavoured hazelnut spread	54g		raw apple	10g
	jams & preserves	48.5g		ground cinnamon	2g
	milk chocolate	51.5g		dark chocolate (70–85% cocoa solids)	24g

BREAKFAST CEREAL (grams of sugar per 100g)

Avoid			Choose		
Honey Nut Cheerios	33g		instant oatmeal	1g	
low-fat fruit granola	32g		puffed rice	0g	
natural granola with oats, wheat & honey	20g				

BREAD, BISCUITS, BUNS & CAKES (grams of sugar per 100g)

Avoid			Choose		
sponge cake	37g		pumpernickel or rye bread	0.5g	
chocolate-chip cookies	33g		wholewheat pitta bread	less than 1g	
bagel	6g		frozen puff pastry	less than 1g	
French bread or sourdough	5g		plain crackers	less than 0.5g	
sliced white bread	4g				

LOW-FAT AND 'DIET' FOODS (grams of sugar per 100g serve)

Avoid			Choose		
non-fat fruit yoghurt	19g		plain whole milk yoghurt	5g (lactose)	
low-calorie mayonnaise	4g		regular mayonnaise	less than 1g	

*Total sugar content according to the USDA National Nutrient Data Base for Standard Reference. Read labels carefully as sugar content varies between brands.

11

SAVOURY FOOD (grams of sugar per 100g)

Avoid		Choose	
barbecue sauce	33g	canned tomatoes in juice	3g
tomato ketchup	21g	plain salted crisps	less than 0.5g
tomato & basil pasta sauce	7g		
ready-made sweet & sour cooking sauce	19g		
barbecue flavour potato crisps	5g		

ALCOHOLIC DRINKS (grams of sugar per 100ml)

Avoid		Choose	
crème de menthe (72 proof)	49g	gin, rum, vodka, whiskey, beer, sake	0g
coffee liqueur (63 proof)	40g	red & white table wine	less than 1g
sweet dessert wine	8g		

TAKEAWAY AND FAST FOOD (grams of sugar per 100g)

Avoid		Choose	
Chinese restaurant sweet & sour chicken	11g	Chinese restaurant chicken chow mein	2g
fast-food chain cheeseburger	6g	deep-fried and battered fish fillet	under 0.5g
fast food chain coleslaw	12g	fast-food chain French fries	less than 0.5g

ALTERNATIVES TO SUGAR IN COOKING

Try replacing added sugar with the following naturally sweet options –
they'll also boost flavour and compensate for lack of sweetness. Experiment
with quantities according to the recipe and personal taste.

UNSWEETENED APPLE SAUCE
Use instead of sugar in baked
goods like biscuits, muffins
and cakes, adding more of the
dry ingredients to compensate
if necessary. Also spoon over
yoghurt or cereal instead of
honey or sugar.

DRIED FRUIT
Contains lots of concentrated
sugar but also valuable
nutrients (counts as one
of the recommended five
daily servings of fruit and
vegetables). Blitz fresh dates to
a paste in a food processor and
use instead of sugar in baked
goods. If using dried dates or
other dried fruit, soak in water
before blitzing. Add more
dry ingredients in baking to
compensate if necessary.

MASHED BANANA
Use instead of sugar in dense
bakes like carrot cake and
banana loaf. Riper bananas are
sweeter, or use roasted bananas.

CINNAMON
Adds gentle sweetness
and flavour. Lovely stirred
into coffee.

NUTMEG
Adds gentle sweetness
and flavour.

GROUND FENNEL SEEDS
Adds gentle sweetness
and flavour.

VANILLA
Scraped beans from the pod,
vanilla powder or unsweetened
vanilla extract add sweetness.
Note: some brands of vanilla
extract contain added sugar.

COCONUT OIL
Adds a hint of sweetness when
frying food or used in baking
instead of vegetable oil or
butter. Add a little to smoothies.

COCONUT MILK
Adds gentle sweetness when
used instead of dairy milk in
shakes, smoothies and cooking.

ALMOND MILK
Adds gentle sweetness
and creaminess to shakes,
smoothies, and lovely in baking.
Opt for unsweetened versions.

SIMPLE WAYS TO BYPASS SUGAR

Sugar is such a large part of our everyday diet that often we don't even realise we're consuming it. By paying attention to the sugar content of what we eat, and making simple dietary adjustments, it's easy to dramatically reduce our intake.

START by cutting out or reducing intake of sugary beverages, especially fizzy drinks and fruit juice, which are the most damaging ways to consume sugar. Drink milk, water, vegetable juice or diluted fruit juice instead. Try gradually reducing sugar in hot beverages until you don't add any.

WHEN baking, reduce quantities of sugar in recipes by one-third to one-half. Make puddings, cakes and biscuits a treat rather than part of your everyday diet.

RESEARCH the total sugar (especially fructose) content of the food and drink you consume – quantities vary significantly between brands. Read labels carefully.

cook from scratch

processed food .... JUMP the SUGAR ⤳ cook from scratch

AVOID processed food, which is loaded with added sugar, and cook more from scratch, especially sauces, dressings and breakfast cereals. Shop in the outer aisles of the supermarket where fresh produce is generally sold.

buy full-fat versions

low-fat products .... JUMP the SUGAR ⤳ buy full-fat versions

AVOID low-fat products – manufacturers load these with added sugar to make them palatable. Instead of fruit-flavoured yoghurt, for example, buy plain yoghurt and swirl through fruit puree.

choose unsweetened snacks

sugary snacks .... JUMP the SUGAR ⤳ choose unsweetened snacks

EAT lots of small meals, as many as six a day, to reduce the temptation to snack on sugary food. Identify your weaknesses and find unsweetened substitutes. For example, if you like sweet biscuits with your coffee, keep nuts or sugar-free crackers by the kettle.

low-sugar fruit

eating fruit .... JUMP the SUGAR ⤳ low-sugar fruit

FRESH fruit is a healthy choice, but contains lots of sugar, especially fructose, so enjoy in moderation and go for the less sugary kinds. The adjacent list includes fruit with less than 10g sugar per 100g, from lowest to highest. Choose cans of fruit in unsweetened juice rather than syrup.

FRUIT

with less than 10g sugar per 100g:

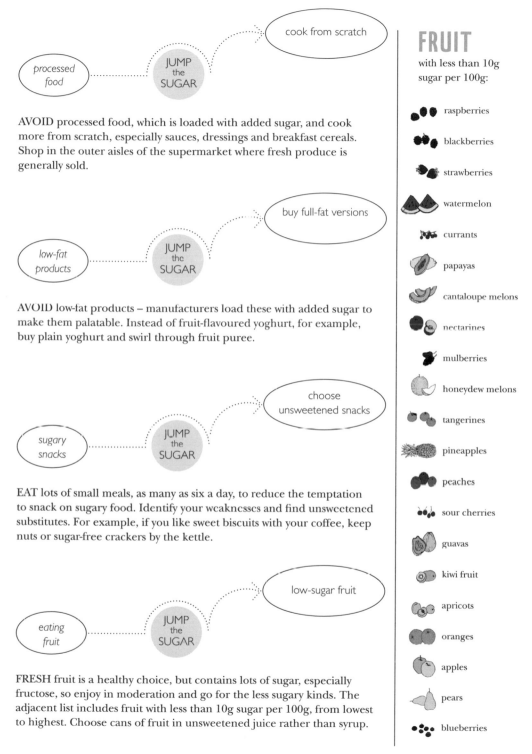

- raspberries
- blackberries
- strawberries
- watermelon
- currants
- papayas
- cantaloupe melons
- nectarines
- mulberries
- honeydew melons
- tangerines
- pineapples
- peaches
- sour cherries
- guavas
- kiwi fruit
- apricots
- oranges
- apples
- pears
- blueberries

BASICS

Processed food is loaded with added
sugar, so try these recipes for basic store
cupboard items to avoid the sugar you
don't even realise you're eating.

Ketchup • BBQ sauce • Apple sauce
Mayonnaise • Peanut butter • Blueberry jam
Chocolate spread • Pastry • Yoghurt
Vinaigrette • Creamy dressing • Wholemeal loaf

KETCHUP

Makes: about 250ml • Time: 1 hour

YOU NEED
2 tablespoons olive oil • ½ onion, chopped • ½ red pepper, chopped
½ red apple, chopped with skin on • a generous pinch of fine sea salt
1 garlic clove, chopped • 2 tablespoons tomato purée
2 ripe tomatoes, about 250g, chopped • 60ml passata
2 tablespoons red wine vinegar • a pinch of cayenne pepper
½ teaspoon ground cinnamon • 2 cloves • ¼ teaspoon celery salt • 1 bay leaf

Heat the oil in a large pan and gently cook the onion, pepper and apple
for 15 minutes, stirring often. Season with salt, add the garlic and cook for
5 minutes more. Stir in the tomato purée, then add the remaining ingredients
and gently cook, covered, for 15 minutes. Stir now and then. Uncover and cook
for 5 minutes more. Discard the bay leaf and blitz the sauce in a food processor
until smooth. Add more salt and pepper or vinegar to taste, then push through
a sieve. Store in an airtight container in the fridge.

BBQ SAUCE

Makes: about 500ml • Time: 1 hour

YOU NEED

400ml passata • 1 onion, chopped • 2 garlic cloves, chopped

2 tablespoons tomato purée • 2 teaspoons Dijon mustard

3 tablespoons apple cider vinegar • 1 tablespoon vegetable oil

2 tablespoons sweet smoked paprika • ½ teaspoon cayenne pepper

1 teaspoon sea salt flakes • ½ teaspoon liquid smoke (optional)

80g unsweetened pineapple chunks • 60ml unsweetened pineapple juice

1 tablespoon Worcestershire sauce (or soy sauce), or to taste

1 tablespoon raisins • about 400ml chicken stock, plus extra if needed

Blend together all the ingredients except the stock in a food processor until smooth. Transfer to a pan, add a splash of the stock, and gently simmer, uncovered, for 45 minutes. Stir regularly, adding a splash of stock each time to maintain a sauce-like consistency as the mixture reduces. Add more salt or pepper to taste. Store in an airtight container in the fridge.

APPLE SAUCE

Makes: 500g • Time: 1–3 hours

YOU NEED

1kg sweet apples, cored and chopped with skin on

2 teaspoons ground cinnamon (optional)

Preheat the oven to 170°C/325°F/Gas 3. Place the apples in an ovenproof
pan and roast, covered, for about 1 hour, or until completely soft. Stir halfway
through. Alternatively, cook in a slow cooker on high for 3 hours. Transfer to a
blender or food processor, add the cinnamon (if using) and blitz until smooth.
Store in an airtight container in the fridge.

MAYONNAISE

Makes: about 250g • Time: 10 minutes

YOU NEED

2 egg yolks • 1 tablespoon lemon juice, plus extra to taste
a generous pinch of sea salt flakes • 250ml vegetable oil
2 tablespoons olive oil • 1 heaped teaspoon Dijon mustard
sea salt flakes

Beat together the egg yolks, lemon juice and salt with electric beaters or a whisk until creamy. Add the oils in a very thin stream while beating constantly until the mixture is thick and pale. Stir in the mustard and add more lemon juice or salt to taste. Store in an airtight container in the fridge.

PEANUT BUTTER

Makes: about 400g • Time: 10 minutes

YOU NEED
400g unsalted roasted peanuts • sea salt flakes, to taste
1 tablespoon vegetable oil

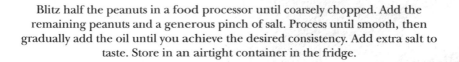

Blitz half the peanuts in a food processor until coarsely chopped. Add the
remaining peanuts and a generous pinch of salt. Process until smooth, then
gradually add the oil until you achieve the desired consistency. Add extra salt to
taste. Store in an airtight container in the fridge.

BLUEBERRY JAM

Makes: about 600g • Time: 45 minutes

YOU NEED
800g blueberries, rinsed and stalks removed • 2 tablespoons lemon juice
400ml unsweetened grape juice

Place the blueberries in a heavy pan, mash with a potato masher, then stir in the lemon juice and grape juice. Bring to the boil, then reduce the heat and simmer, uncovered, for 30–40 minutes, or until thick and reduced to the desired consistency. Pour into sterilised jars and store in the fridge.

CHOCOLATE SPREAD

Makes: about 200g • Time: 10 minutes

YOU NEED

100g skinless blanched hazelnuts • 1 teaspoon vanilla extract
60g pitted fresh dates • 3 tablespoons unsweetened cocoa powder
1 tablespoon hazelnut oil • 1 teaspoon milk powder
a pinch of fine sea salt • 2–3 tablespoons coconut cream

Gently toast the hazelnuts in a dry frying pan until fragrant and starting to brown. Leave to cool a little, then transfer to a food processor and blitz to a paste. This takes a while so stick with it. Add the remaining ingredients and blitz until very smooth and creamy, adding as much coconut cream as necessary to achieve the desired consistency. Store in an airtight container in the fridge.

PASTRY

Makes: enough for 1 x 25cm tart or covered pie • Time: 40 minutes

YOU NEED
250g plain flour, plus more for dusting • a pinch of salt
125g cold butter, diced • 1 egg

Place the flour, salt and butter in a food processor and pulse until the mixture resembles breadcrumbs. Add the egg and pulse again until the mixture comes together. Tip onto a lightly floured work surface and shape into a smooth disc without kneading. Wrap in cling film and chill for 30 minutes before rolling.

YOGHURT

YOU NEED

2 litres full-fat milk • 120ml live natural yoghurt at room temperature

Place the milk in a lidded, ovenproof pan and slowly heat to 80°C/175°F.
Remove from the heat and cool to 45°C/115°F. Pour 200ml of the milk into a
mixing bowl, stir in the yoghurt, then pour the mixture back into the milk pan.
Stir, cover and wrap the pan in 2 tea towels. Switch on the oven light (don't
switch the oven on), place the pan inside and leave for 4–8 hours, or until
set to the desired consistency. For Greek-style yoghurt, tip into a muslin-lined
colander set over a bowl and leave to drain until thick and creamy.
Store in an airtight container in the fridge.

VINAIGRETTE

YOU NEED
2 tablespoons red or white wine vinegar • 1 teaspoon Dijon mustard
sea salt flakes • freshly ground black pepper • 60ml vegetable oil
2 tablespoons mild extra virgin olive oil

Place all the ingredients in a screw-top jar and shake vigorously until combined.
Store in an airtight container in the fridge.

CREAMY DRESSING

Makes: about 200ml • Time: 5 minutes

YOU NEED

150ml natural yoghurt (p34) • 2 tablespoons sour cream or crème fraîche
½ garlic clove, crushed • 1 tablespoon chopped fresh dill, chives,
flat-leaf parsley or a mixture • ½ teaspoon Dijon mustard
2 tablespoons cider vinegar or white wine vinegar
90ml mild extra virgin olive oil

Place all the ingredients in a screw-top jar and shake
until completely combined. Store in an airtight container in the fridge.

WHOLEMEAL LOAF

250g strong wholemeal flour • 250g strong white flour, plus extra for dusting
1 teaspoon fine sea salt • 2 teaspoons fast-action dried yeast
250g vitamin C tablet, crushed to a powder • 1½ tablespoons unsalted butter,
melted and cooled • 300–400ml warm water • vegetable oil, for oiling

Preheat the oven to 200°C/400°F/Gas 6. Combine the flours, salt, yeast and vitamin C. Add the butter and stir in enough warm water to make a sticky dough. Knead for 1 minute on a floured work surface and shape into a ball. Leave to rest in a covered, oiled bowl for 2 hours, or until doubled in size. Knock back the dough, shape into a ball and leave to rest for 15 minutes. Oil a large loaf tin. On a lightly oiled work surface, flatten the dough into a rectangle the length of the tin. Tightly roll up the dough and place in the tin seam-side down. Cover with a tea towel and set aside for 45 minutes–1 hour until risen to the top of the tin. Bake for 40 minutes until golden. Cool on a wire rack before cutting.

BREAKFAST

Sugary breakfast cereals are a major
source of added sugar for many people.
Try these unsweetened options to reduce
your added sugar intake.

Mango & carrot smoothie • Fruit spritzer
Beetroot smoothie • Date & oat thickshake
Peanut butter & chocolate shake
Berry ripple porridge • Granola • Luxe muesli
Bircher muesli • Pancakes with sautéed peaches
Rye & berry waffles • Banana French toast
Strawberry cream cheese toast

MANGO & CARROT SMOOTHIE

Makes: about 500ml, depending on consistency • Time: 5 minutes

YOU NEED
80g carrots, peeled • 50g parsnips, peeled
180g mango flesh, chopped

If using a powerful blender or food processor, roughly chop the carrots and parsnips, otherwise grate the vegetables. Place in the bowl of the blender or food processor, add the mango and blitz until smooth. With the motor running, gradually add enough water to achieve the desired consistency. Serve immediately.

FRUIT SPRITZER

Serves: 2 • Time: 5 minutes

YOU NEED

1 peach, finely chopped • a handful of grapes

a handful of mint leaves, plus extra to serve • ½ teaspoon grated fresh ginger

1 lemon, zest finely grated and thinly sliced

a handful of frozen berries • sparkling water

In a small bowl, mix together the peach, grapes, mint, ginger and lemon zest. Press the mixture against the side of the bowl with a wooden spoon to slightly crush the fruit and release the juices. Divide the mixture between 2 glasses. Add the frozen berries, mint and lemon slices. Top up with sparkling water and serve immediately.

BEETROOT SMOOTHIE

Serves: 2 • Time: 5 minutes

YOU NEED

2 medium cooked beetroots, quartered • ½ small fennel bulb, chopped
a large handful of baby spinach • a handful of frozen berries
1.5cm piece fresh ginger, peeled and chopped, plus extra to taste

Place all the ingredients in a blender, add 125ml water and blitz on high power until smooth. Add more water if needed to achieve the desired consistency. Serve immediately.

DATE & OAT THICKSHAKE

Serves: 2 • Time: 5 minutes

YOU NEED

1 large banana • 60g pitted fresh dates

60g rolled oats • 350ml almond or dairy milk, plus extra to taste

2 tablespoons unsweetened cocoa powder • a pinch of ground cinnamon

Place all the ingredients in a blender and blitz until smooth. Add extra milk to achieve the desired consistency. Serve immediately.

PEANUT BUTTER & CHOCOLATE SHAKE

Serves: 2 • Time: 5 minutes

YOU NEED

1 large banana • 350ml almond or dairy milk, plus extra to taste

120g unsweetened peanut butter (p26)

1 heaped tablespoon unsweetened cocoa powder

Place all the ingredients in a blender and blitz until smooth and creamy,
adding enough milk to achieve the desired consistency. Serve immediately.

BERRY RIPPLE PORRIDGE

Serves: 4 • Time: 25 minutes

YOU NEED

300g strawberries • 40g pitted fresh dates • 30g quinoa flakes
30g rye flakes • 30g spelt flakes • 30g buckwheat groats or flakes
40g pinhead oatmeal • 1 tablespoon chia seeds
a pinch of fine sea salt • 500ml almond or dairy milk • pistachios, to serve

Blitz the strawberries and dates together in a food processor until smooth, adding a splash of water to loosen if needed. Set aside. In a saucepan, combine the flakes, groats, oatmeal, chia seeds, salt and milk. Bring to the boil, stirring constantly, then reduce the heat and simmer for 20 minutes. Stir frequently during this time, adding a splash of water now and then to maintain your preferred consistency. The flakes should be tender and the mixture thick and creamy when done. Serve with the strawberry sauce swirled through and scatter with pistachios.

GRANOLA

Serves: 8+ • Time: 40 minutes

YOU NEED

200g rolled oats • 200g quinoa flakes or other flaked grains
250g mixed nuts such as almonds, pistachios, pecans and macadamias,
roughly chopped • 65g pumpkin seeds
½ teaspoon fine sea salt • 1½ teaspoons ground cinnamon
100ml melted coconut oil • 250ml unsweetened apple juice
1 large egg white • 25g desiccated coconut
125g mixed dried fruit of choice, chopped

Preheat the oven to 150°C/300°F/Gas 2 and line a baking tray with baking paper. In a large bowl, combine the oats, flakes, nuts, seeds, salt, cinnamon, coconut oil and apple juice. Mix well. Whisk the egg white until frothy and stir into the mixture. Spread out in the prepared baking tray and bake for 15 minutes, then mix in the coconut. Bake for 15–20 minutes more, or until golden. Leave to cool on the tray, then add in the dried fruit. Store in an airtight container.

LUXE MUESLI

Serves: 8 • Time: 5 minutes

YOU NEED
120g rolled oats • 120g quinoa flakes • 120g spelt or rye flakes
60g almonds, chopped • 60g pecan nuts, chopped • 60g pistachios, chopped
30g pumpkin seeds • 45g sunflower seeds • 1½ tablespoons chia seeds
2 tablespoons sesame seeds • 30g coconut flakes • 60g sultanas
30g dried cherries • 60g dried mango, chopped • 30g goji berries
90g dried apricots, chopped • 2 teaspoons ground cinnamon
2 teaspoons vanilla extract • 1 teaspoon nutmeg • a pinch of fine sea salt

In a large mixing bowl, stir together all the ingredients until evenly distributed. Store in an airtight container.

BIRCHER MUESLI

Serves: 4–6 • Time: 10 minutes, plus several hours soaking

YOU NEED
180g rolled oats • 60g buckwheat, rye or spelt flakes
40g mixed seeds (like chia, linseed, sunflower and pumpkin) • 2 apples, cored
and grated • 400ml unsweetened apple juice • 500ml milk
1 teaspoon vanilla extract • 1 teaspoon ground cinnamon
Optional extras to serve: chopped dried fruit, fresh berries,
nuts and/or Greek-style yoghurt (p34)

Combine all the ingredients except the optional extras in a mixing bowl and
stir to combine. Transfer to a lidded container and chill in the fridge for several
hours, ideally overnight. Serve topped with optional extras of choice.

PANCAKES WITH SAUTÉED PEACHES

Serves: 4 generously • Time: 20 minutes

125g wholemeal flour • ½ teaspoon baking powder • a pinch of fine sea salt

1 teaspoon melted coconut or vegetable oil, plus extra for frying

1 egg • 150ml almond or dairy milk, plus extra if needed

1 teaspoon vanilla extract • 6 ripe peaches

3 tablespoons unsalted butter, plus more if needed

1 teaspoon ground cinnamon • 180ml unsweetened apple juice

In a mixing bowl, stir together the flour, baking powder and salt. Stir in the
1 teaspoon oil, the egg, milk and vanilla. Grate 2 of the peaches and stir into the
batter. Heat a little oil in a frying pan and add heaped spoonfuls of batter. Cook
until golden underneath, then flip and cook for 30 seconds more. Transfer to a
plate and cover with foil. Halve, stone and slice the remaining peaches, then fry
them in the butter until soft. Add the cinnamon, then pour in the apple juice,
stirring as it bubbles and thickens. Add more butter or apple juice if needed to
make a sauce. Serve the pancakes with the peaches and sauce spooned over.

RYE & BERRY WAFFLES

Serves: 4–6 • Time: 25 minutes

YOU NEED

300g blueberries • 100g rye flour

100g plain flour • ½ teaspoon baking powder

½ teaspoon bicarbonate of soda • 200ml milk

2 eggs, lightly beaten • 50g unsalted butter, melted and cooled

1 teaspoon vanilla extract • 120g Greek-style yoghurt, plus extra to serve

vegetable oil, for brushing • chopped hazelnuts, to serve

Blitz 200g of the blueberries in a food processor to make a sauce. Set aside.
In a mixing bowl, stir together the flours, baking powder and bicarbonate
of soda. Make a well in the centre and stir in the milk, eggs, butter, vanilla
and yoghurt. Gently stir in the remaining blueberries. Heat the waffle iron,
brush with oil and pour batter into the compartments. Cook according to the
machine instructions, transferring the waffles to a wire rack as you go. Serve
topped with yoghurt, the blueberry sauce and hazelnuts.

BANANA FRENCH TOAST

Serves: 2 • Time: 15 minutes

YOU NEED

2 large eggs • 2 tablespoons unsalted butter, melted

a generous pinch of fine sea salt • a pinch of mace

a pinch of nutmeg • a pinch of ground cloves

¼ teaspoon ground cinnamon • finely grated zest of 1 orange

2 tablespoons orange juice • 1 large ripe banana, mashed

2 tablespoons cream cheese • 4 thick slices good-quality white bread

2 tablespoons chopped pecan nuts (optional) • 1 tablespoon vegetable oil

In a shallow bowl, whisk together the eggs, half of the melted butter, the salt, spices, orange zest and orange juice. Set aside. In a separate bowl, beat together the banana and cream cheese. Spread 2 of the bread slices with the banana mixture, sprinkle with the pecans (if using), and top with the remaining bread to make sandwiches. Gently press down to seal. Heat the remaining butter and the oil in a frying pan until foaming. Dip the sandwiches in the egg mixture, ensuring each side is soaked but not enough to disintegrate. Fry for 2 minutes until crisp and golden underneath, then flip and cook for 1 minute more. Serve immediately.

STRAWBERRY CREAM CHEESE TOAST

Serves: 4 • Time: 10 minutes

YOU NEED
4 thick slices sourdough or country-style bread • 200g cream cheese
200g strawberries, hulled and sliced • ground cinnamon, for sprinkling

Toast the bread. Meanwhile, beat the cream cheese to loosen. Spread thickly on
the hot toast, top with strawberry slices and sprinkle with cinnamon.
Serve immediately.

SNACKS

Replace sugary treats with these good-for-you snacks. Dried fruit does contain concentrated sugars as well as nutrients, so consume in moderation.

Cinnamon popcorn • Lime & chilli almonds
Fruit roll-ups • Berry dip with fruit crudités
Whipped banana toast • Apple crisps
Orange & saffron grissini • Doughnut balls
Apricot & coconut balls • Chocolate energy bars
Fruit & nut bars • Chocolate raisins
Stuffed dates • Freezer fudge

CINNAMON POPCORN

Serves: 2-4 • Time: 10 minutes

YOU NEED

50g unsalted butter, melted • 2 teaspoons vanilla extract
1½ tablespoons vegetable oil • 50g popcorn kernels
ground cinnamon, to taste

Beat together the butter and vanilla, then set aside. In a heavy-lidded pan, heat the oil over a medium–high heat and add 4 of the popcorn kernels. Cover. When the kernels have popped, remove from the heat and add the remaining kernels. Shake, return to the heat and cover. Cook, shaking occasionally, until there are 3 seconds between pops. Remove from the heat, shake the pan and wait for stray kernels to pop. Pour over the vanilla butter, sprinkle with cinnamon and toss. Serve immediately.

LIME & CHILLI ALMONDS

Makes: about 350g • Time: about 1 hour

YOU NEED
60ml lime juice • finely grated zest of 2 large limes
1 tablespoon melted coconut oil • 1 teaspoon sweet smoked paprika
1 teaspoon hot chilli powder • 1 teaspoon ground cinnamon
2 teaspoons fine sea salt • about 12 drops Tabasco chipotle sauce, or to taste
300g blanched almonds

74

Preheat the oven to 120°C/250°F/Gas ½ and line 1 or 2 baking sheets with baking paper (you might need to cook the nuts in batches). Mix together all the ingredients except the almonds in a bowl. Add the almonds and toss to coat. Spread out in a single layer on the prepared baking sheets and bake for 45 minutes–1 hour, stirring halfway, until golden brown. Keep an eye on them to prevent burning. Leave to cool on the tray before serving.

FRUIT ROLL-UPS

Makes: 2 sheets measuring 30 x 25cm • Time: 6–8 hours

YOU NEED

800g ripe stone fruit such as plums, peaches or apricots, chopped with skin on
a squeeze of lemon • 1 banana (optional)

Line 2 baking sheets with baking paper. Place the fruit in a pan with the squeeze of lemon and a splash of water. Gently simmer, stirring occasionally, until the fruit releases its juice. Reduce the heat to low, cover and cook for 15 minutes, stirring occasionally, until very soft. Blitz in a blender or food processor until smooth. Taste for sweetness, add some or all of the banana if needed, and blitz again. Preheat the oven to 50°C/140°F. Pour the mixture onto the prepared baking sheets and spread out evenly to a thickness of 3–5mm. Place in the oven for 6–8 hours, or until firmed into a gel that peels off the paper easily. To serve, cut into strips and roll up.

BERRY DIP WITH FRUIT CRUDITÉS

Serves: 4–6 • Time: 10 minutes

YOU NEED

180g frozen mixed berries, defrosted • 100g pitted fresh dates
3 tablespoons melted coconut oil • 3 tablespoons coconut milk
grated zest of ½ orange • chopped fruit, for dipping

Place the berries and dates in the bowl of a food processor and blitz until
smooth. Add all the remaining ingredients except the chopped fruit and blitz
until amalgamated and smooth. Serve with the chopped fruit for dipping.

WHIPPED BANANA TOAST

Makes: 2 slices • Time: 10 minutes

YOU NEED
20g coconut oil • 1 banana • 1 teaspoon ground cinnamon
a pinch of ground nutmeg • 2 slices wholemeal bread • mixed berries, to serve

Melt the coconut oil in a frying pan over a medium–high heat. Slice the
banana, add to the pan and cook until soft and caramelized on both sides.
Sprinkle over the cinnamon and nutmeg, and cook for 1 minute more.
Transfer to a mini food processor and blitz until smooth. Alternatively, mash to
the desired consistency. Toast the bread, then spread with the whipped banana.
Serve immediately, with the berries.

APPLE CRISPS

Makes: about 60 • Time: 4–5 hours

YOU NEED

4 apples • 1 teaspoon ground cinnamon

Preheat the oven to 110°C/225°C/Gas ¼ and line a large baking sheet with baking paper. Very thinly slice the apples crossways, ideally using a mandoline. Arrange in a single layer on the prepared baking sheet and sprinkle with the cinnamon. Cook for 4–5 hours – the exact time will depend on the thickness of the slices – flipping halfway through. The crisps should be pale brown and starting to harden. Switch off the oven and leave the crisps inside until cool. Store in an airtight container.

ORANGE & SAFFRON GRISSINI

Makes: about 40 • Time: 1 hour, plus 2 hours 40 minutes proving

YOU NEED

90ml orange juice, warmed • a pinch of saffron threads, chopped
10g fast-action dried yeast • about 200ml warm water
450g plain flour, plus extra for dusting • 1 teaspoon fine sea salt
finely grated zest of 1 orange • vegetable oil, for oiling and brushing

Combine the juice and saffron in a small bowl and set aside. In another bowl, combine the yeast and warm water and set aside for 5 minutes. In a mixing bowl, combine the flour, salt and zest, then stir in the yeast and saffron mixtures. Bring the dough together, tip onto a floured work surface and knead for 10 minutes. Set aside in a covered, oiled bowl for 20 minutes. On an oiled work surface, stretch the dough into a circle, fold in half then in half again and shape into a ball. Return to the oiled bowl, cover and set aside for 2 hours. Preheat the oven to 200°C/400°F/Gas 6. Line 2 large baking sheets with baking paper and flour a chopping board. Punch back the dough, tip onto the board and roll into a rectangle 5mm thick. Cut into 2cm strips and gently roll into pencil shapes. Transfer to the prepared baking sheets, brush with oil and set aside for 20 minutes, bake for 20 minutes, then cool on a wire rack.

DOUGHNUT BALLS

Makes: 24 • Time: 40 minutes, plus 2–3 hours proving

YOU NEED

1½ teaspoons fast-action dried yeast • 60ml warm water • 300g plain flour
1 teaspoon fine sea salt • about 750ml vegetable oil for deep-frying,
plus extra for oiling • blueberry jam (p28) or berry dip (p78), to serve

Combine the yeast and warm water and set aside for 5 minutes. In a mixing
bowl, mix together the flour and salt. Add the yeast mixture, then gradually
stir in up to 120ml water to make a sticky dough. Turn out onto a lightly oiled
work surface and briefly knead. Transfer to an oiled bowl, cover with cling film
and leave somewhere warm for 2–3 hours, or until doubled in size. Knock back
the dough, knead for 1 minute, divide into 24 equal pieces, and roll into balls.
Heat the 750ml vegetable oil to 175°C/350°F. Deep-fry the balls in batches for
about 6 minutes, turning them over in the oil until golden. Transfer to kitchen
paper with a slotted spoon. Serve hot, with the jam or dip for dipping.

APRICOT & COCONUT BALLS

Makes: about 50 • Time: 15 minutes

YOU NEED

120g rolled oats • 70g unsweetened peanut butter (p26) • 100g ready-to-eat
dried apricots • 40g puffed rice • 20g desiccated coconut, plus extra for rolling
80–100g unsweetened apple sauce (p22)

Blitz the oats to a powder in a food processor, then add the peanut butter,
apricots, puffed rice and coconut. Blitz until combined. Add 80g of the apple
sauce and blitz until the mixture comes together, adding more apple sauce if
needed. Roll heaped teaspoonfuls of the mixture into balls, then roll in the
coconut. Store in an airtight container in the fridge.

CHOCOLATE ENERGY BARS

Makes: 16 squares • Time: 15 minutes, plus 2 hours chilling

YOU NEED

400g pitted fresh dates • 60ml melted coconut oil

2 teaspoons vanilla extract • 40g unsweetened cocoa powder

125g ground almonds • a pinch of fine sea salt

1 heaped tablespoon golden flaxseeds • 40g pistachios, roughly chopped

40g walnuts, roughly chopped • 50g dried blueberries

50g sunflower seeds • 2 tablespoons desiccated coconut

Blitz the dates in a blender to a paste. Add the coconut oil, vanilla and cocoa
powder, and blitz again until smooth. Tip into a bowl, add the almonds,
then bring the ingredients together with a wooden spoon or clean hands.
Gradually work in all the remaining ingredients except the coconut until evenly
dispersed. Line a 20cm square brownie tin or container with foil and tip in the
mixture. Press in firmly with the back of a spoon, sprinkle with coconut and
lightly press in. Chill for 2 hours, or until set, then cut into squares. Store in an
airtight container in the fridge.

FRUIT & NUT BARS

Makes: 16 squares • Time: 10 minutes, plus 2 hours chilling

YOU NEED

225g pitted fresh dates • 150g rolled oats • 80g raisins

50g dried apples • 50g skinless blanched hazelnuts • 25g ground almonds

25g walnuts • 3 tablespoons unsweetened apple sauce (p22)

1½ teaspoons ground cinnamon • a pinch of ground nutmeg

Place all the ingredients in the bowl of a food processor and blitz to produce a well-combined and slightly coarse, sticky mixture. Firmly press into a 20cm square tray or brownie tin lined with cling film. Chill for 2 hours, or until set, then cut into squares. Store in an airtight container in the fridge.

CHOCOLATE RAISINS

Makes: about 350g • Time: 10 minutes, plus 2 hours chilling

YOU NEED

100g dark chocolate made from 100% cocoa solids, grated

80g coconut oil • 4 tablespoons double cream

1 teaspoon vanilla extract • 200g raisins

Line a baking sheet with greaseproof paper. Place the chocolate and
coconut oil in a heatproof bowl set over a pan of gently simmering water. Stir
occasionally until melted together. Remove the bowl from the pan and stir
in the cream and vanilla, then the raisins. Set aside for a few minutes for the
mixture to thicken slightly. Pour onto the prepared baking sheet, ensuring
the raisins are in a single layer. Chill in the fridge for 2 hours, or until the
chocolate has hardened. Break into pieces to serve. Store in
an airtight container in the fridge.

STUFFED DATES

Makes: 24 • Time: 15 minutes

YOU NEED
120g soft goats' cheese • 1 teaspoon finely grated orange zest
50g nuts, such pistachios, almonds and/or walnuts, finely chopped
240g pitted fresh dates

Beat the goats' cheese and orange zest until smooth and creamy. Stir in the nuts until well combined. Gently pull the dates apart and stuff with the cheese mixture using a small spoon or knife. Press the dates closed and serve immediately.

FREEZER FUDGE

Makes: about 24 bars • Time: 15 minutes, plus 1–2 hours freezing

YOU NEED
400g pitted fresh dates • 120g tahini
120ml double cream • a generous pinch of salt

Line a 20cm square freezer-proof container or brownie tray with cling film. Blitz the dates to a paste in a food processor, then add the tahini, cream and salt. Blitz again until smooth and creamy. Pour into the prepared tray, spread out with a spatula and smooth the top. Transfer to the freezer for 1–2 hours, or until set, then cut into rectangles. Store in an airtight container in the fridge.

BAKED

The following recipes prove that it's possible to bake delicious sweet goodies without using added sugar.

Date & spelt crackers • Blueberry & apple muffins
Seedy peach muffins • Banana loaf
Chocolate torte • Carrot cake
Raspberry & almond focaccia
Sweet potato scones • Peanut butter cookies
Chocolate oatmeal cookies • Thumb print biscuits

DATE & SPELT CRACKERS

Makes: 16 • Time: 30 minutes, plus 25 minutes freezing and cooling

YOU NEED
60g plain flour, plus extra for dusting • 60g wholemeal flour
½ teaspoon fine sea salt • 60g cold unsalted butter, diced
2 tablespoons spelt flakes • 40g pitted dried dates, chopped • 1 egg yolk

Preheat the oven to 180°C/350°F/Gas 4 and line 1 large or 2 small baking sheets with baking paper. Place the flours and salt in a mixing bowl and rub in the butter with your fingertips. Mix in the spelt and dates, then the egg and 1 tablespoon water. Turn out onto a floured work surface and lightly knead for 1 minute, then shape into a sausage 6cm in diameter. Wrap in greaseproof paper and freeze for 20 minutes. Cut the dough into 5mm slices and transfer to the baking sheet(s). Bake for 12–15 minutes until pale gold. Leave on the baking sheet(s) for 5 minutes, then transfer to a wire rack to cool. Store in an airtight container.

BLUEBERRY & APPLE MUFFINS

Makes: 12 • Time: 40 minutes

YOU NEED

150g plain flour • 50g wholemeal flour

1½ teaspoons baking powder • 2 teaspoons ground cinnamon

a pinch of fine sea salt • 75g unsalted butter, melted and cooled

75g unsweetened apple sauce (p22) • 100g Greek-style yoghurt (p34)

100ml milk • 1 teaspoon vanilla extract • 1 medium egg • 150g blueberries

Preheat the oven to 200°C/400°F/Gas 6 and line a 12-hole muffin tin with paper cases. In a mixing bowl, mix together the flours, baking powder, cinnamon and salt. In a jug, whisk together the butter, apple sauce, yoghurt, milk, vanilla and egg. Pour the wet mixture into the dry ingredients and stir just enough to combine – a few lumps are fine. Fold in the blueberries. Spoon into the prepared muffin tin and bake for 20 minutes, or until golden and an inserted skewer comes out clean. Transfer to a wire rack to cool.

SEEDY PEACH MUFFINS

Makes: 9 • Time: 40 minutes

YOU NEED
140g ground almonds • 40g plain flour • 20g desiccated coconut
2 teaspoons ground cinnamon • 1½ teaspoons baking powder
a pinch of fine sea salt • 20g sunflower seeds • 2 large eggs
½ ripe banana, mashed until smooth • 4 tablespoons melted coconut oil
4 tablespoons unsweetened apple sauce (p22) • 1 teaspoon almond essence
160g ripe peaches, diced, plus extra for topping

Preheat the oven to 180°C/350°F/Gas 4 and line 9 holes of a muffin tin
with paper cases. In a mixing bowl, mix together the almonds, flour, coconut,
cinnamon, baking powder, salt and sunflower seeds. In a jug, whisk together
the eggs, banana, oil, apple sauce and almond essence. Pour the wet mixture
into the dry ingredients and stir until just combined. Fold in the 160g peaches.
Divide between the paper cases and top with more peaches. Bake for 20
minutes, or until an inserted skewer comes out clean. Cool on a wire rack.

BANANA LOAF

Makes: 1 large loaf • Time: 60 minutes

YOU NEED

vegetable oil, for oiling • 225g plain flour, plus extra for dusting

100g unsalted butter • 120g unsweetened apple sauce (p22)

2 large eggs • 40g Greek-style yoghurt (p34)

1 teaspoon vanilla extract • 300g ripe bananas, mashed

1 teaspoon bicarbonate of soda • a pinch of salt

1 teaspoon allspice • 2 tablespoons milk

125g raisins • 75g walnuts, chopped

Preheat the oven to 180°C/350°F/Gas 4. Oil and flour a 12 x 25cm loaf tin, or equivalent. In a mixing bowl, beat together the butter and apple sauce until creamy – don't worry if the mixture looks a little curdled. Gradually beat in the eggs, then the yoghurt, vanilla and bananas. Combine the flour, bicarbonate of soda, salt and allspice. Gradually stir the dry ingredients into the banana mixture, alternating with the milk. Fold in the raisins and walnuts. Pour into the prepared tin, smooth the top and bake for 40 minutes, or until an inserted skewer comes out clean. Leave in the tin for 5 minutes before turning out onto a wire rack to cool.

CHOCOLATE TORTE

Serves: 6–8 • Time: 45 minutes

YOU NEED

140g ground almonds • 45g unsweetened cocoa powder

½ teaspoon baking powder • a pinch of fine sea salt

200g pitted prunes • 80ml Pedro Ximénez or other sweet sherry (or grape juice)

2 tablespoons olive oil • 2 teaspoons vanilla extract • 3 large eggs

Preheat the oven to 170°C/325°F/Gas 3 and oil a 20cm spring-form cake tin.
Mix together the almonds, cocoa, baking powder and salt. Set aside.
Place the prunes and alcohol or grape juice in a small pan and simmer until
2 tablespoons of the liquid remain. Set aside to cool, then transfer to the bowl
of a food processor. Add 120ml water, the olive oil and vanilla. Blitz to a paste.
Transfer to a mixing bowl, add the eggs and beat until light and creamy. Add
the almond mixture and stir until smooth. Pour into the prepared tin and bake
for 25 minutes until cool to touch. Cool in the tin for a few minutes before
releasing. Serve warm or at room temperature.

CARROT CAKE

Serves: 6–8 • Time: 1 hour

YOU NEED

150ml sunflower oil, plus extra for oiling • 125g plain flour, plus extra for dusting • 125g wholemeal flour • 1 teaspoon baking powder • 1 teaspoon bicarbonate of soda • a pinch of fine sea salt • 2 teaspoons ground cinnamon ½ teaspoon ground ginger • 50g walnuts, chopped • 70g sultanas 150g bananas, mashed • 3 large eggs, lightly beaten 150g pineapple, chopped • 200g carrots, grated

---

FOR THE ICING

100g unsalted butter, softened • 150g cream cheese 2 teaspoons vanilla extract • 1 teaspoon ground cinnamon 90–135g unsweetened apple sauce (p22) according to taste

Preheat the oven to 180°C/350°F/Gas 4 and oil and flour a 22cm spring-form cake tin. In a mixing bowl, combine the flours, baking powder, bicarbonate of soda, salt, spices, walnuts and sultanas. In a jug, combine the bananas, oil and eggs. Pour the wet ingredients into the flour mixture and stir until just combined. Fold in the pineapple and carrots. Pour into the prepared tin and bake for 30–40 minutes until springy to touch. Meanwhile, beat together the butter, cream cheese, vanilla, cinnamon and apple sauce. Chill until needed. When the cake is completely cool, spread the icing over the top.

RASPBERRY & ALMOND FOCACCIA

Serves: 6–8 • Time: 45 minutes, plus 1 hour 20 minutes proving

YOU NEED

400g strong white bread flour, plus extra for dusting • 100g fine semolina flour

2 teaspoons fennel seeds (optional) • a pinch of fine sea salt

7g fast-action dried yeast • 300ml warm water • olive oil, for oiling and drizzling

250ml unsweetened red grape, pomegranate or apple juice

about 200g raspberries • a handful of sliced almonds

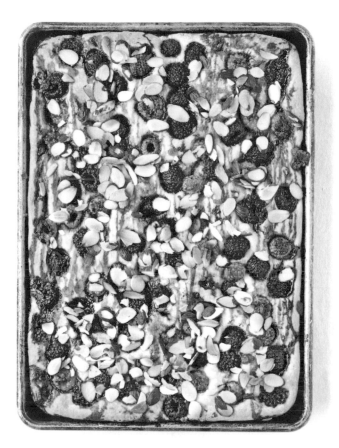

In a mixing bowl, stir together the flours, fennel seeds (if using) and salt. In a separate bowl, combine the yeast and warm water and set aside for 5 minutes. Make a well in the centre of the dry ingredients and stir in the yeast mixture to form a dough. Briskly knead for 10 minutes – it will be sticky at first but avoid using flour on the work surface. Set aside somewhere warm in a covered, oiled bowl for 1 hour. Meanwhile, simmer the juice until reduced to 60ml (about a quarter of the original volume), then set aside to cool. Oil a 20 x 30cm baking tray, tip in the dough and flatten out to fill the tray. Push raspberries into the top, pour over the reduced juice, sprinkle with the almonds and drizzle with oil. Cover with a tea towel and set aside for 20 minutes. Preheat the oven to 220°C/425°F/Gas 7, then bake for 20 minutes. Cool on a wire rack for 15 minutes before serving.

SWEET POTATO SCONES

Makes: 8 • Time: 40 minutes

YOU NEED

275g self-raising flour, plus extra for dusting • 1½ teaspoons allspice
a pinch of fine sea salt • a pinch of ground nutmeg
80g cold unsalted butter, diced • 100g dried peach, apricot or nectarine
(or a mixture), chopped • 150g roasted sweet potato flesh, mashed
1 large egg • 75ml milk, plus extra if needed and for brushing

Preheat the oven to 220°C/425°F/Gas 7. In a mixing bowl, stir together the flour, allspice, salt and nutmeg. Rub in the butter with your fingertips, then stir in the dried fruit. In a separate bowl, mix together the sweet potato, egg and 4 tablespoons of the milk, then add to the dry ingredients. Mix to form a soft dough that holds together without crumbling. On a floured work surface, shape into a disc 2.5cm thick and stamp out circles with a 7cm cutter. Bring together the trimmings, roll out and stamp out more circles. Repeat until the dough is used up. Transfer to a baking sheet, brush with milk and bake for 12 minutes until golden. Serve warm with cream and blueberry jam (p28).

PEANUT BUTTER COOKIES

Makes: 12 • Time: 30 minutes

YOU NEED

100g plain flour • 50g wholemeal flour

100g ground almonds • ½ teaspoon bicarbonate of soda

2 teaspoons ground cinnamon • a pinch of fine sea salt

75g unsalted butter, softened • 1 large egg, beaten

4 tablespoons peanut butter (p26) • 100g sultanas, chopped

2 tablespoons milk, or more or less as needed

Preheat the oven to 180°C/350°F/Gas 4. Stir together the flours, almonds, bicarbonate of soda, cinnamon and salt. Set aside. Beat the butter until pale and fluffy, then gradually beat in the egg and peanut butter. Stir in the flour mixture and the sultanas, adding just enough milk to make a soft dough. Roll heaped tablespoons of the mixture into balls and flatten into discs 5mm high with the tines of a fork. Bake for about 10 minutes until pale gold, then transfer to a wire rack to cool.

CHOCOLATE OATMEAL COOKIES

Makes: about 14 • Time: 30 minutes

YOU NEED

100g pitted fresh dates • 60g unsweetened cocoa powder • 30g ground almonds

3 egg whites • 1 tablespoon melted coconut oil

40g rolled oats • 30g desiccated coconut

Preheat the oven to 170°C/325°F/Gas 3 and line a baking sheet with baking paper. Place the dates, cocoa, almonds and egg whites in the bowl of a food processor and blitz until smooth. Add the coconut oil and pulse to combine. Transfer to a mixing bowl and stir in the oats and coconut. Roll tablespoons of the mixture into balls, place on the prepared baking sheet and flatten into 6cm discs. Bake for 5 minutes, flip and cook for 5 minutes more. Cool on the tray.

THUMB PRINT BISCUITS

Makes: about 30 • Time: 40 minutes

YOU NEED

180g unsalted butter • 230g unsweetened apple sauce (p22)

1 egg, lightly beaten • 2 teaspoons vanilla extract

finely grated zest of 1 orange • 90g ground almonds, or more if needed

180g plain flour • ¼ teaspoon fine sea salt

1 teaspoon ground cinnamon • 1 teaspoon ground ginger

about 250g blueberry jam (p28) or other sugar-free jam

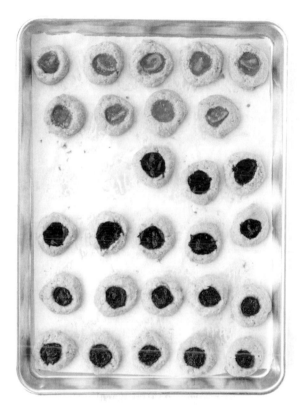

Preheat the oven to 160°C/315°F/Gas 2–3 and line a baking sheet with baking paper. Beat together the butter and apple sauce until creamy – don't worry if the mixture looks curdled. Gradually stir in the egg, then the vanilla and orange zest. Add the almonds, flour, salt and spices, then stir to make a stiff dough-like batter. Add more almonds if too loose. Place tablespoonfuls of the mixture on the prepared baking sheet. Using damp fingers, pat into 5cm discs and make an indentation in the middle. Bake for 20 minutes, or until pale gold. Spoon a teaspoonful of jam onto each biscuit while still warm.

DESSERTS

Everyone loves the occasional sweet treat
to finish off a meal. The following recipes
fit the bill, without containing
any added sugar.

Fruit salad & rosewater dressing
Saucy pears with pecans • Fig & mint syllabub
Chocolate mousse • Berry chia pudding Bread
& butter pudding • Apple & raspberry jelly Fruit
crumble • Apple pie • Blueberry cheesecake
Lime & coconut ice cream • Berry ice cream
Chocolate ice cream • Strawberry ice pops
Melon & apple granita

FRUIT SALAD & ROSEWATER DRESSING

Serves: 4 • Time: 25 minutes

YOU NEED

250g Greek-style yoghurt (p34) • 4 tablespoons chopped mint, plus extra to
serve • 4 tablespoons pomegranate molasses • 1 teaspoon rosewater
700g mixed fruit such as persimmons, plums and figs, chopped
4 tablespoons pomegranate seeds, to serve

Mix the yoghurt and mint together, cover and chill. Meanwhile, for the
dressing, whisk together the pomegranate molasses and rosewater. Place
the fruit in a bowl, toss with half the dressing and set aside for 15 minutes.
Distribute the fruit between bowls, drizzle over the remaining dressing and top
with the yoghurt, pomegranate seeds and mint leaves.

SAUCY PEARS WITH PECANS

Serves: 4 • Time: 20 minutes

YOU NEED

4 firm, ripe pears • 1 tablespoon lemon juice, plus extra to taste
3 tablespoons unsalted butter • 250ml unsweetened pineapple juice
4 tablespoons double cream, plus extra if needed
40g chopped pecans • a pinch of salt

Quarter, core and slice the pears. Toss with the 1 tablespoon lemon juice and set aside. Melt the butter in a frying pan until foaming, add the pears and fry over a medium–high heat until almost tender and starting to caramelise. Add the pineapple juice and stir as it bubbles up, then cook until reduced by half. Lower the heat, stir in the cream and cook to a sauce-like consistency. Stir in the pecans, salt and more lemon juice or cream to taste. Serve immediately.

FIG & MINT SYLLABUB

Serves: 4 • Time: 15 minutes

YOU NEED

400ml double cream • 1 teaspoon ground cinnamon
2 teaspoons vanilla extract • 1 tablespoon Pedro Ximénez sherry (or other
sweet sherry or unsweetened grape juice) • 100ml natural yoghurt (p34)
4 large figs, cut into chunks • 240ml unsweetened grape juice
1 tablespoon chopped mint • 40g walnuts, chopped

Beat together the cream, cinnamon, vanilla and the Pedro Ximénez sherry
to a soft dropping consistency – don't overbeat, as it will thicken more in the
fridge. Stir in the yoghurt, then chill. Place the figs in a bowl and toss with the
240ml grape juice and mint. Set aside for 5 minutes for the flavours to mingle.
To assemble, layer the figs and juice, the cream and the walnuts in glasses and
serve immediately.

CHOCOLATE MOUSSE

Serves: 4 • Time: 10 minutes, plus 3 hours chilling

YOU NEED

200g pitted fresh dates • 400ml thick coconut milk or coconut cream
50g unsweetened cocoa powder • 1 teaspoon vanilla extract
3 tablespoons melted coconut oil • 60g raspberries, plus extra to serve
whipped cream, to serve (optional)

Blitz the dates in a food processor to a paste. Add the remaining ingredients and blitz again until smooth. Pour into 4 ramekins, smooth the tops and chill for at least 3 hours to set. Serve topped with raspberries and cream (if using).

BERRY CHIA PUDDING

Serves: 4 • Time: 10 minutes, plus overnight chilling

YOU NEED
500ml almond or dairy milk • 2 large bananas
2 teaspoons vanilla extract • 80g chia seeds
160g red berries such as rasberries and/or strawberries, chopped

Place the milk, bananas and vanilla in a blender and blitz until smooth. Transfer to a large bowl and stir in the chia seeds. Cover with cling film and chill overnight. Spoon into bowls and serve topped with the red berries. Serve immediately.

BREAD & BUTTER PUDDING

Serves: 4-6 • Time: 40 minutes

YOU NEED

unsalted butter, for buttering and spreading • 8 thin slices wholemeal bread

grated zest of 1 orange • 80g dried figs, chopped

3 large eggs, lightly beaten • 350ml almond or dairy milk

50ml double cream • 1 teaspoon ground cinnamon

2 teaspoons vanilla extract • 150g bananas, mashed until smooth

Preheat the oven to 180°C/350°F/Gas 4 and generously butter a 1.2 litre
baking dish. Butter one side of each slice of bread and cut each slice in half.
Arrange half the bread in the bottom of the baking dish buttered-side up and
scatter half the orange zest and half the figs on top. Arrange the remaining
bread on top and scatter over the remaining zest and figs. Whisk together the
eggs, milk, cream, cinnamon, vanilla and banana, and pour over the bread.
Bake for 30 minutes until golden. Serve warm.

APPLE & RASPBERRY JELLY

Serves: 4 • Time: 15 minutes, plus 6 hours chilling

YOU NEED

250g mixed raspberries

5 gelatine leaves (or enough to set 600ml liquid)

600ml unsweetened apple juice • whipped cream, to serve

Distribute the raspberries between glasses that hold at least 300ml each.
Set aside. Place the gelatine leaves in a heatproof bowl and add enough of
the apple juice to cover. Set aside to soften for 5 minutes. Place the bowl over
a pan of gently simmering water and stir until completely dissolved. Add the
remaining apple juice, stir well, then pour into the glasses with the raspberries.
Chill for 6 hours, or until set. Serve with whipped cream.

FRUIT CRUMBLE

Serves: 4–6 • Time: 30 minutes

YOU NEED

4 red apples, chopped with skin on • 8 ripe plums, chopped

700ml unsweetened white or red grape juice • 120g quinoa flakes

120g rolled oats • grated zest of 2 oranges

2 teaspoons allspice • 2 teaspoons grated fresh ginger

2 teaspoons ground cinnamon • 80g pecan nuts, chopped

¼ teaspoon fine sea salt • 6 tablespoons unsalted butter • cream, to serve

Preheat the oven to 180°C/350°F/Gas 4 and line a baking sheet with baking paper. Place the fruit and juice in a pan and simmer, stirring occasionally, until tender. Strain, reserve the juice, and set aside. Combine the quinoa, oats, orange zest, spices, pecans and salt in a bowl. Melt the butter in a frying pan until foaming, add the quinoa mixture and stir-fry until the butter is absorbed and the mixture starts to caramelize. Add 180ml of the reserved juice and cook, stirring constantly, until absorbed. Spread out on the prepared baking sheet and bake for 5 minutes, or until crisp. Spoon the fruit and reserved juices into bowls and top with the crumble. Serve with whipped cream.

APPLE PIE

Serves: 8 • Time: 1 hour 10 minutes, plus 30 minutes chilling

YOU NEED
1 quantity pastry (p32) • grated zest of ½ orange
60ml unsweetened orange juice • 6 green apples such as Granny Smith apples
2 teaspoons ground cinnamon • ½ teaspoon ground nutmeg
1 teaspoon vanilla extract • 50g raisins
1 tablespoon plain flour, plus extra for dusting
1 egg, lightly beaten with a splash of water

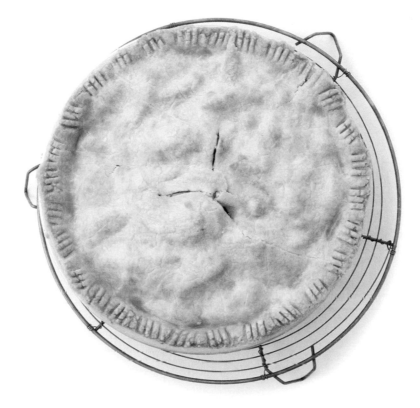

Cut the dough into 2 pieces, one slightly larger than the other. Shape into discs, wrap in cling film and chill for 30 minutes. Place the zest and juice in a bowl. Peel, quarter and core the apples, slice into the orange juice and toss. Mix in the spices, vanilla, raisins and flour. Preheat the oven to 180°C/350°F/ Gas 4. Roll out the large piece of dough and use it to line a 20cm pie tin, allowing some overhang. Add the apples and moisten the dough edge with water. Roll out the small piece of dough to make a lid. Press the edges together with a fork and trim away excess dough. Cut slits in the top, brush with the egg wash and bake for 45 minutes, or until golden. Cool in the tin for 15 minutes before serving.

BLUEBERRY CHEESECAKE

Makes: 4 • Time: 20 minutes, plus 2 hours chilling

YOU NEED

80g rolled oats • 60g pitted fresh dates

80g ground almonds • 3 tablespoons melted coconut oil

a pinch of fine sea salt • 280g cream cheese

2 teaspoons vanilla extract • 250ml double cream

280g blueberry jam (p28) or other sugar-free spread • a handful of blueberries

Place the oats in a food processor and blitz to a powder. Add the dates, almonds, coconut oil and salt, and blitz until combined. Divide between 4 x 10cm cheesecake tins (or a 20cm spring-form cake tin) and press in firmly and evenly with the back of a spoon. Chill. Meanwhile, beat together the cream cheese, vanilla and cream until thick. Spread evenly over the chilled base. Chill for 2 hours, or until set. When ready to serve, spread with the blueberry jam and top with blueberries. Release from the tin and serve immediately.

LIME & COCONUT ICE CREAM

Serves: 4–6 • Time: 20 minutes, plus up to 5 hours freezing

YOU NEED

2 bananas • 450ml coconut cream • 450ml double cream
grated zest of 4 limes • a generous pinch of fine sea salt
4 tablespoons desiccated coconut, lightly toasted

Blitz the bananas in a food processor until smooth and creamy. Transfer to
a mixing bowl and add the coconut cream, cream, zest and salt. Beat until
smooth and creamy, then stir in the desiccated coconut. Pour into an ice-cream
maker and churn according to the machine instructions. Alternatively, place
in a freezer-proof container and freeze for 3–4 hours, then blitz in a food
processor. Freeze for 1 more hour then blitz again just before serving.

BERRY ICE CREAM

Serves: 4 • Time: 5 minutes

YOU NEED
500g frozen mixed berries • 80–120g pitted fresh dates, according to taste
120ml coconut cream or single cream

Place all the ingredients in the bowl of a food processor, blitz until smooth
and creamy and serve immediately. Alternatively, transfer to the freezer for
30 minutes for a firmer ice cream. Store in the freezer for longer if needed,
but blitz again until creamy before serving.

CHOCOLATE ICE CREAM

Serves: 2 • Time: 5 minutes

YOU NEED
2 frozen bananas • 2 tablespoons unsweetened cocoa powder
60ml coconut cream

Chop the bananas, transfer to the bowl of a food processor and blitz until broken up. Add the cocoa and coconut cream, and blitz until creamy. Serve immediately. Alternatively, transfer to the freezer for longer, if needed, but blitz again until creamy before serving.

STRAWBERRY ICE POPS

Makes: 4–6 • Time: 10 minutes, plus up to 8 hours freezing

YOU NEED
500g strawberries, hulled • 80g pitted fresh dates
100ml double cream • a few drops of rosewater, or to taste

Blitz the strawberries and dates in a blender, then add the remaining
ingredients and blitz until combined. Pour into ice pop moulds and freeze for
5–8 hours, or until frozen. Run the moulds briefly under warm water to release.

MELON & APPLE GRANITA

Serves: 4 • Time: 10 minutes, plus 4 hours freezing

YOU NEED
750g chopped honeydew melon • 225g unsweetened apple sauce (p22)
juice of 1–2 limes • a handful of mint leaves

Place the melon and apple sauce in a blender and blitz until smooth. Add lime juice and mint to taste, and blitz again. Pour the mixture into a loaf tin or metal container that will fit into the freezer. Freeze for 2 hours, or until the mixture is frozen around the edges. Scrape and stir the mixture with a fork, then return to the freezer. Repeat stirring and scraping every 30 minutes for 2 hours, or until the mixture is formed of ice crystals. Serve immediately.

GLOSSARY

Artificial sweeteners – chemically manufactured substances including aspartame, sucralose and saccharine designed to mimic the sweetness of sugar. Highly controversial, some critics claim they cause a range of health problems, while advocates say they can help control weight alongside a low-calorie diet.

Blood sugar – the amount of glucose present in the blood.

Carbohydrates – also known as 'carbs', are a source of energy. When eaten, the body converts them into glucose (blood sugar), which is used to fuel bodily functions and activity. Sugar is a type of carbohydrate.

Empty calories – food that supplies energy but little or no nutrition.

Fibre – a type of carbohydrate only found in food that comes from plants. Essential for optimum health, sources of fibre include vegetables with the skin on, wholegrain bread, wholegrain pasta and pulses.

Fructose – a simple sugar found in many fruit and vegetables, and only processed in the liver. Some experts believe fructose behaves more like fat than other carbohydrates and that excessive consumption can lead to sugar cravings, over-eating and health problems.

Glucose – also known as dextrose, is the body's preferred source of energy. It is also known as blood sugar, as it circulates in the blood.

Insulin – a hormone produced by the pancreas that helps the body store and use glucose.

Lactose – a type of sugar found in milk and other dairy products. It is regarded as a healthy sugar as it contains no fructose.

Starch – a form of carbohydrate made up of many sugar units bonded together. Starchy foods include bread, rice, potatoes and pasta.

Stevia – a naturally occurring sweetener and sugar substitute extracted from the leaves of the Stevia plant. It has no calories and is up to 200 times sweeter than sucrose.

Sucrose – commonly known as table sugar or added sugar, it is made up of fructose and glucose molecules.

Type 1 diabetes – an autoimmune condition, often inherited, where the pancreas does not produce any insulin, the hormone responsible for controlling blood sugar levels.

Type 2 diabetes – a condition where the pancreas does not produce enough insulin, or the body's cells don't react to insulin, the hormone responsible for controlling blood sugar levels. The rapid worldwide rise in the incidence of Type 2 diabetes is linked to obesity, lack of exercise and an increase in unhealthy diets.

Xylitol – a naturally occurring chemical found in plant material widely used as a sugar substitute.

INDEX

My thanks to Catie Ziller and the team for all the hard work that has made this book so beautiful. It can be a tricky task to make all the pieces of the puzzle come together and they succeeded brilliantly. Special thanks go to Alice Chadwick for her gorgeous illustrations.

Thanks go to lookslikewhite ceramics at www.lookslikewhite.com for their lovely ceramics. Other stunning pieces came from Canvas Home, ABC Carpet & Home, CB2, Muji and Kaufmann mercantile.

I am also grateful to Magimix UK for the loan of their Cuisine 5200XL food processor, which was a huge asset while testing all the recipes.

Finally, big hugs to Adam, Ruby and Ben – my family, test team and most valued critics. Thanks especially to Ruby for devising the Date & oat thickshake recipe, and for Ben's suggestions on muffin ingredients.

Sugar Free by Sue Quinn

First published in 2015 by Hachette Books (Marabout)
This English hardback edition published in 2016 by Hardie Grant Books

Hardie Grant Books (UK)
5th & 6th Floors
52-54 Southwark Street
London SE1 1UN
www.hardiegrant.co.uk

Hardie Grant Books (Australia)
Ground Floor, Building 1
658 Church Street
Melbourne, VIC 3121
www.hardiegrant.com.au

British Library Cataloguing-in-Publication Data. A catalogue record for this book is available from the British Library.

ISBN: 978-1-78488-042-2

Publisher: Catie Ziller
Author: Sue Quinn
Photographer: Victoria Wall Harris
Design & illustration: Alice Chadwick
Food stylist: Vivian Lui
Assistant food stylist: Cybelle Tondu

For the English Hardback edition:
Publisher: Kate Pollard
Senior Editor: Kajal Mistry
Cover image: iStock
Cover Design: Hardie Grant Books
Cover Colour Production by P2D

Printed and bound in China by 1010

10 9 8 7 6 5 4 3 2 1